STEPPING
into
TRUST

A Poetic Journey of Recovery

BRENDA RAUSCH

WESTBOW
PRESS®
A DIVISION OF THOMAS NELSON
& ZONDERVAN

WestBow Press books may be ordered through booksellers or by contacting:

WestBow Press
A Division of Thomas Nelson & Zondervan
1663 Liberty Drive
Bloomington, IN 47403
www.westbowpress.com
1 (866) 928-1240

Interior Image Credit: Theresa Dearon

ISBN: 978-1-9736-4189-6 (sc)
ISBN: 978-1-9736-4190-2 (hc)
ISBN: 978-1-9736-4188-9 (e)

Library of Congress Control Number: 2018911898

Print information available on the last page.

WestBow Press rev. date: 10/25/2018

12/9/2018

Many blessings to you on your journey!
May you have courage & trust in God
every step of the way to live the life
you imagine each day ~

Wishing you peace,
Brenda
Rausch

This book is dedicated to my fellow travelers on the journey.

Contents

Acknowledgments

Words feel inadequate to express how grateful I am for all the people who supported and inspired me to share my story and poetry in a book. I have been blessed beyond measure.

- To my family, especially my incredible husband, Tom, who loved me throughout this journey.
- To Theresa for her generous contribution of beautiful artwork.
- To Marie, who helped me give birth to this book through her skilled, gentle guidance.
- To others who encouraged me to continue when I felt like abandoning the project, especially Lindsay, Jeanine, Heather, Annetta, Jack, and Ray.
- To all my friends who came alongside me with their prayers, words of hope, strength, and comfort.
- To God be all glory, honor, and praise!

Introduction

The poems in this book were birthed over several years, with the majority coming after I celebrated my one-year anniversary of freedom from alcohol. I use the term *birthed* because of the mental and emotional labor pains I felt when writing them. Initially I was calling them hairballs because it felt like a primal form of purging. Then I came to the realization that I needed to honor the process. Inspiration came from a higher source, from God, helping me heal through a form of expression with which I was not familiar.

If someone would have predicted that I was going to write poetry in this quantity and eventually put them out there for the world to see, I would not have believed them. I have come to believe that God can do far more than we ask or imagine in our lives. It's amazing what we can do when we step out in faith. God sure does work in mysterious ways. Transformation and change is a primary activity in the process of recovery.

These poems were an integral part of my recovery journey. They helped me heal. My hope and prayer are that they will be helpful to you on your journey as well.

The Poetry

Around my one-year sober anniversary,
All these poems spill out of me.

The words come forth as I approach places of wonder and pain.
Pondering the next phrase with great regard, it feels a bit insane.

The curious gift of prose and rhyme,
Feeling both amazed and guilty, taking the time.

It has been said that vulnerability is the birthplace for change and creativity.
Then sharing them with others must surely have some utility.

Share them as I dare is the direction
For help with feelings of connection.

I don't know what else to do
But to share them with you.

I don't understand how this can be;
In college English I got a D.
Poetry? Really? Me?

These poems are not coming from me! I declare.
They are born from another place—but where?

Will it help these remnant feelings of despair?
Only God knows when it will end … Should I care?

The Awareness

My poems reflect the depth of pain I've carried,
Trauma of my past I hoped was dead and buried.

Over a couple of months, they rose to the surface,
Confirming my wounded spirit was part of their purpose.

In these places of hurt, I frequently reside;
With an open heart I am asked to abide.

Of one thing I can be sure:
Only with this awareness can healing occur.

Awareness can bring significant pain,
A precursor of enormous gain.

With willingness to trust the process of discovery,
I continue this challenging journey of recovery.

Addiction and the Past

We know that suffering produces perseverance; perseverance, character; and character, hope. And hope does not put us to shame, because God's love has been poured out into our hearts through the Holy Spirit, who has been given to us.

—Romans 5:3–5

I lost my mother to cancer during adolescence. My father died five years later from a massive stroke. My father was in recovery from alcoholism and suffered from a debilitating mental illness for as long as I can remember. I continue to struggle with accessing my feelings from childhood, but what I do recall is being scared a lot. My childhood experiences carried forward to adulthood.

I've been an overachiever, people pleaser, and perfectionist for most of my life. I didn't do anything I couldn't be good at. Go big or go home. All or nothing. This trait has suited me well in career advancement and not so well in other areas of my life. Unfortunately, a consequence of the desire to achieve has been a struggle with overworking and burnout (aka work addiction). Over the years, I rationalized and minimized my work addiction. Society rewards work addiction with rock star status. On the surface, the consequences may appear not as severe as with chemical addiction. As I explored my situation, I learned that work addiction is common for many people from chemically dependent and dysfunctional homes, and it has some of the same symptoms and effects as chemical addiction. It is a distraction and "medicates" emotional pain.[1] I began connecting how much work had become a friend, and the thoughts about it were friends as well. During the time I spent working, I had good energy. The problem was that when I stopped working for any significant period, I had withdrawal symptoms. I couldn't sleep and had obsessive work thoughts, low mood, anxiety, and irritability.

By the grace of God, I found out about a residential codependency treatment program that specialized in the issues I experienced. I returned from that program and followed their directions by attending individual and group therapy. I joined a couple of self-help groups that focused on relationships and work addiction. I'd have a period of abstinence and then slip back into overworking. I tried to stay open to learning but really wanted to shield myself from pain and loss. My instinct was to allow the numbing quality of depression to wash over me.

A couple of years after I returned from the treatment program, I was diagnosed with major depression. This illness came on quite quickly, and the symptoms were getting worse by the day. I used alcohol to cope with the symptoms, but it wasn't helping any longer. Alcohol had become my new drug of choice. I admitted to my therapist what was going on, and she wanted me to go to treatment. On Mother's Day of that year I woke up with new clarity that I needed to get honest. I told my husband I needed more structured help than what I was getting with weekly therapy. Arrangements were made, and off to rehab I went the next day.

The Toddler and the Teenager

"It's not fair," the toddler said,
"that my daddy has a sick head.

I'm scared of the yelling.
I'm scared of being alone.
I'm scared he might not come back home.

I am trying to be a good girl,
To not cause trouble.

This hurts!"

"It's not fair," the teenager said,
"that my mom is dying in bed.

I hate the pain.
I hate the loss.
I hate being afraid of the future.

I am tired of being a good girl,
And I feel like causing trouble.

This stinks!"

The Eyes

The innocent, trusting eyes untouched by the harshness of life
Change to eyes of abandonment hardened by betrayal, loss, and strife.

The eyes of a mom dying alone in her bed,
With no one to hold her hand or wipe her head.

The eyes of an orphaned child in a photograph,
Not knowing when she again will laugh.

The expectant eyes of the man coming for communion,
Only to be denied the anticipated reunion.

It is said that the eyes are mirrors to the soul.
What I see reflected often are dark, suffering holes.

Glimpses of numbed pain remain
In the penetrating look that rocks my spirit to its core.
Those are the eyes full of unshed tears that can weep no more.

The Unknowing

"I don't know where I'm going," she said as she slowly slipped away.
But at sixteen, I had places to go and didn't want to stay.
I touched her foot; she flinched
as if trying to keep the pull of an unknown force at bay.

And as I looked into her sad, tired eyes, I saw she felt betrayed.
With this feeling forever burned into my memory, I left,
not knowing the price to be paid.
God, why did you let me leave? I should have stayed!

The Darkness

The darkness descended like a cloud,
A thick, black, suffocating shroud.

Loneliness and despair beyond belief
From which I was desperately seeking relief.

For a while, I was able to hide behind my mask
Until that too became an impossible task.

I hoped maybe it would go away,
For what would others have to say?

A voice inside cried, *Get help before it's too late.*
This doesn't have to be your fate.

Hitting bottom one morning, I came to believe,
Asked for that help, and was granted a reprieve.

The Premonition

I had a dream several years ago that eventually led me down another road.
It was so real and vivid, I can still feel the weight of its heavy load.

The dream foretold the future given my then-current direction.
A clear sign of a much-needed course correction.

Bottom-line message: I was killing myself with frenetic activity,
Overly focused on distracting productivity.

I know I've been an overachiever all my life.
Now my obsessive, one-track mind was causing great strife.

Sometimes it takes such experiences of painful insight
For me to surrender and see the light.

The Void

Tears escape into the void,
The void where words are useless.
Only feelings to deny,
To run from and hide.

Resistance, depression, denial, repression—
All fancy words for trying to avoid the pain
That comes to me at every turn,
Like ants trying to dodge the rain.

Cool smile on the outside but crumbling within.
This is the mask I wear, the game I play.
To experience need without relief
Is the torture doled out today.

I am awakening to my true self, you say.
Trust that I will heal with time.
I desperately want to believe you and pray,
But the void draws me ever in.

The Longing

The longing for relief from God knows what.
My attempts to fill the hole not quite good enough.

Forever striving to hit the sweet spot of life
Eventually turns to suffering, disappointment, and strife.

"Make room for grief," you say.
"Feel this pain you have today."

"Nothing can help" has been my belief.
So nothing is done, effectively trapping relief.

The Shoe

Mother, father, lover, friend,
Dreams, hopes, relationships end.

Waiting for the next shoe to fall,
The next loss appearing like a pall.

I cannot control the future or change the past.
Somehow I think my lot has been cast.

Anticipation of some future tragedy
Had become my lifelong strategy.

The Obsession

It felt uncontrollable in the end;
About this, I don't try to pretend

To understand how my thinking
So quickly became obsessed with drinking.

It washed over me like a flood,
Like a vampire hungry for blood.

I only drank a little bit,
So why was it so hard to quit?

Certainly not enough to get addicted.
I will surely not always be restricted.

It is just the depression, I concluded.
I'm not that sick or deluded.

Allergy of the body and obsession of the mind—
These are the relentless ties that bind.

I do remember way back how it started,
And now it's just best that we parted.

It's always been an intractable love affair.
I wish I could say it's totally over, but I still care.

The Beef

I don't like this anger and sadness that aren't new.
It's just under the surface. Not sure what to do.

It feels old and not completely my own.
The seeds of a mother's pain and loss unintentionally sown.

In her daughter they now reside,
Occasionally fed by life's turbulent tide.

It is so easy to pass on to others this agonizing feeling of abandonment and grief,
A harsh reality that has been my ongoing beef.

The Pictures of the Past

Swirling and vague, the same old thoughts appear.
Desperate to get them out so my head can clear.

I'm so tired of thinking, wanting to finally feel
The pain of the past that still seems so real.

I keep recalling the high school picture of my mother: a beautiful, young,
unsuspecting soul—
Having no idea what she was in for as life took its toll.

I can sure relate to how she must have felt
About the injustice of the cards she was dealt.

My life is nowhere near as hard,
Yet lingering fear seeps in to torment and bombard.

Early Recovery

Pain stretches us to our limits, generally forcing us to look
for guidance from others and it pushes us to consider new
choices in our present situation.

—Karen Casey, *Each Day a New Beginning*[2]

Reentering the world after spending time in a safe, structured
environment was very challenging. I had to figure out how to
live without using behaviors and chemicals to numb my feelings.
At the same time, I needed to take responsibility for the consequences
of my addictive behavior. This included the delicate task of mending
relationships. Fortunately, God provided a method for this work to occur.
I jumped into a local recovery program with both feet and gradually grew
stronger from the love and support it offered. I found wonderful, new,
sober friends and started building my sober support network. I continued
to attend individual and group therapy. After a few months into my sober
life, my husband and I found we needed help to heal our relationship, and
so we engaged a couple's therapist.

I didn't know how sick I was until I started to get well. I didn't know
what wonderful resources and support were available. All I had to do was
get out of my comfort zone and be willing to take the risk. I needed to
learn to be okay with asking for help. I needed to learn from others how
to stay sober.

The Journey

It's been a year of healing.
Still my soul continues reeling.

In the deep dark places, the pain still hides,
Occasionally surfacing with feeling tides.

Many of the paths feel untested and brand-new,
Questioning how to navigate the uncharted waters I come to.

Some shaky bridges to cross and rapids to forge.
Do I know how to maneuver the deep, treacherous gorge?

"One day at a time. Trust the process," I hear.
But how do I do that with all this fear?

Today with one small step, again I begin.
But how does it end, and do I win?

The Seed

Waking up a seed that has been planted.
A gift to my true self cannot be taken for granted.

Like a tender sapling, it shoots up toward the sky.
Who am I to question why
This growth is happening in my life.
Inspiration as sharp as a surgeon's knife.

Cutting off all the unneeded shoots
To allow more nourishment to the brand-new roots.

The pruning helps the tree to bear fruit and grow strong,
Just as it takes patience for pain to become a song.

The Choice

Right choice makes for right action.
Does that ultimately lead to greater satisfaction?

One step at a time and day by day,
Lots of learning along the way.

Today I'm willing to trust my inner voice
To lead me to the right choice.

The Steps

1. Admitted powerlessness ... My life taken by a thief.
2. Came to believe. ... I was looking for relief.
3. Turn it over ... does this take belief?
4. Inventory ... way too business, not much fun.
5. Admitted wrong ... again? I want to run.
6. Was willing to heal ... my lifelong goal.
7. Asked God for help ... to heal my soul.
8. More lists ... to reach satisfaction.
9. Made amends to people ... true courage and humility in action.
10. Continued to do inventory ... dare to be vulnerable, a daily task.
11. Sought through prayer and meditation ... only his will to ask.
12. Authenticity and service ... willingness to drop the mask.

The Hope

This word *hope* has walked with me for a while.
At times it feels like a hundred thousand miles.

Hope has become a mantra
To heal from some old trauma.

Even though at times I can't feel you,
Especially when the storms of life ensue,

I look for you in pictures and art
To remind me that we are never apart.

On my body, I've chose to carry you
In the form of a simple tattoo.

So, when I am at the end of my rope and think I can't cope,
I can turn to you again, my faithful friend ... my hope.

The Honoring

Honor my pain, the therapist said.
My initial reaction: "Are you crazy in the head?"

To infer this is something I can attain
Feels totally and completely insane.

I want to push the pain away,
Or ignore it to keep it at bay,

Or distract myself with another thought
That takes me away from feeling distraught.

Still, I do know he was revealing
A pathway to my emotional healing.

Praying about it for now is the best I can do.
Actually doing it will take a major breakthrough.

The Muck

I feel like I'm in the muck.
Wow, I hate being stuck!
My first thought is "Yuck!"
Have I finally run out of luck?
Anger that I can't seem to tuck.
Can I let that go like water off a duck?
Or push it away as fast as a hockey puck?
Or do I try to embrace it instead of buck?

The Roller Coaster

Sometimes life is like a wild roller coaster ride in the dark.
The unpredictable ups, downs, twists, and turns tempt me to disembark.

The expectation that what goes up must come down
Permeates my heightened senses all around.

It brings feelings of fear to the fore,
Ripping into the partially healed sore.

To hang on and be willing to enjoy the ride,
And not worry about the downward slide,

Is the challenge I am asked to pursue—
The attitude that will ultimately see me through

The Dragonfly

She climbs up the lily stem to the water's surface.
It's not an easy journey, but necessary for life's continued purpose.

As the tiny creature rests on the lily pad, a miraculous change takes place:
She turns into a glorious dragonfly with iridescent wings like fine lace.

Having found a new freedom, she joins her friends soaring in the bright
sunshine.
So too, through the gift of recovery, we are transformed by the power of
the divine.

The Scorecard

When playing sports over the years,
I harbored many fears.

Always chosen last on the team in sixth grade,
Entrenching shame is the price I paid.

I tried hard but could not throw the ball,
Learning if I can't be good enough,
I'd rather not do it at all.

Now fast forwarding to the present,
Connecting the dots to current events.

I still assume others are keeping track
Of the talents and motivation I lack,
So they must pick up the slack.

Perfectionistic and competitive to my core.
Aha—new awareness that perhaps I'm the one keeping score!

The Paint

"It's like watching paint dry," my soul declares with conviction.
Boredom forever seeping in with no sign of eviction.

Lacking motivation and interest in the work I do,
Longing for the passion to begin anew.

Feeling like a step child without a home,
My heart and interest continue to roam.

No matter. I continue to watch and wait without end.
God only knows when my ambition will mend.

Cravings and Triggers

Watch and pray that you will not fall into temptation. The spirit is willing, but the flesh is weak.

—Mark 14:38

When I completed the treatment program, I decided I didn't need to attend a twelve-step recovery group because I questioned whether my alcohol use was really a problem. I thought the problem was simply the depression, and I was feeling much better. I fantasized that maybe I could even drink again someday. I was advised by my therapist to not drink at least for a year. I hadn't really thought of drinking since I'd completed rehab; the cravings had passed after about a week in the program. I told one of my friends on the three-month anniversary of my sobriety that I didn't need a self-help group at that time but would consider it if I felt the need. I was going it alone again!

Well, the need showed up the very next day after I made that statement, with early morning cravings for alcohol that hit me hard. In my mind, the choice was to drink or surrender and ask for help from others. After some deep soul searching, I decided to put courage in place of fear and venture to a local self-help meeting.

The Hole

There is never enough to fill the hole,
The hole that lives inside my soul.

The cavern is too big; still I try
The hungry ghost to satisfy.

Try again and again and yet again in vain.
The next new thing to ease the pain.

What drives me on in this belief?
The futile promise of some relief?

Still, there is never enough to fill the hole,
The hole that lives inside my soul.

The Plan

It was a covert operation, the plan I was conceiving
As I sat quietly in prayer and contemplated leaving.

It would only be a little bit, just enough to get some relief
From the torturous thoughts that were gnawing at me like an unseen thief.

No one would ever have to know, I reasoned.
I surely can hide this away for a season.

But *I* will know, the answer quickly followed,
And the guilt will haunt me for many tomorrows.

The mantra "Maybe not right now"
Got me through the
Craving.

Stay the course, my dear.
Your sobriety is worth saving!

The Guests

Weekend guests are coming for a visit.
A special day for my daughter, and they want to be in it.

I have a role to play and much to do,
To be a good host when the festivities ensue.

The adult beverages have been purchased.
The desire to drink has again surfaced.

This craving I hope to contain—
Still I can't hide all the pain.

As irritability seeps through the cracks,
I fervently pray, "God, please help me to relax."

The Using Dream

The craving was profound in my dream.
I wanted it so bad I could scream.

I thought I'd only have a little nip.
What would be the harm of just a sip?

Instead, I took a big gulp immediately after the pour,
Conflicted with both a sense of relief and an intense hunger for more.

Without stopping I downed the large glass, not thinking of my plight.
Suddenly the red wine that remained turned milky white.

I was curious and wondered about the significance.
Maybe a sign of implicit innocence?

The guilt that followed as I awoke took my breath away,
And the feeling of desire mingled with remorse lingered throughout
the day.

The Desire

The cravings still come frequently, and the triggers are everywhere.
At times I feel my sobriety hasn't got a prayer.

Sight, smell, sound, thought—"It's all over," I cry.
Impossible to get away from the temptations, so why even try?

Tired of all the family drama;
It's such unending bad karma.

No wonder I want to drink,
To hide away so I don't have to think.

Difficult to suppress this irritation
As I continue to attempt heartfelt conversation.

Why is it so hard for my loved ones to understand?
Wow, it would be so cool if they could just lend a hand.

Rather than fight against my process of healing,
Perhaps it's fear of change that keeps everyone reeling.

The Dragon

The dragon has been awakened once more.
Painful rumination seeps out of every pore.

After two years, I am seriously thinking about letting my sobriety go.
The dragon is truly a cunning and powerful foe.

I've asked for help in all the ways I know how.
The next seemingly impossible task is to surrender now

And have willingness to trust that God is really there
To pull me out of the dragon's lair.

The Box

I feel trapped at every turn.
Is there something else I should learn

About the container closing me in?
Seems as though I just can't win.

It would be so easy to resort to drinking.
Instead, I'm trying to change my way of thinking,

To come to believe there's a reason,
And I will find out in due season

The purpose of the box keeping me stuck,
Confirming I haven't really run out of luck.

In the meantime, I will pray and reach out as best I can
To other fellow travelers who understand.

Dealing with Emotions: Fear and Anger

For the Spirit God gave us does not make us timid, but gives us power, love and self-discipline.

—2nd Timothy 1:7

Part of the recovery process is getting in touch with emotions that have been numbed by using. As I explored my emotions, I was struck by how much fear and doubt were present and got in the way of what God wanted for me. Fear of not being noticed, validated, acknowledged. Wanting out of the corner I'd put myself in. I was sick of hiding, putting on masks, worrying about what people think, trying to be what I think they want me to be all the time. As a child, I tried to not get in the way as best I could. I tried to not cause any more trouble for my mom and family. "Just get out of the way," was my mode.

The stuff in my mind usually is much worse than reality. If I can be brave enough to let anxious dark thoughts see the light of day, I am better for it, and I feel better. That means I need to write it down or tell someone else about it. Sometimes I'm not sure I want to feel better. It's the idea of worrying and obsessing about the devil I know versus the devil I don't that may follow. I struggled with this need to worry. I had this irrational feeling that somehow worry was protecting me.

Anger was present too. Initially I was afraid to feel angry, and to admit I was angry. I finally see the woundedness behind the anger. The desire to protect, to close in, was significant during the encounters. Staying open is incredibly difficult. When I am open, I feel vulnerable and exposed. In early recovery I struggled with deep feelings of abandonment in daily encounters with others. Keeping isolated is a protective strategy. I knew how to put on the mask. I have been doing that for much of my life. Now the question was, how do I take it off? I had the feeling of constantly being judged by others. I really didn't know how real this was. It was hard to admit this struggle, and it made me very sad.

The Injustice

Why not me? It's not fair!
This lament surfaced, and I really don't want to care.

Today I feel ignored, abandoned, and left out.
I just want to hide and pout.

The age-old story of the haves and have-nots—
Ugly resentment that seals my lot.

This is the way my life works.
Fear of rejection constantly lurks.

I hate this attitude and negativity;
It doesn't help and only makes it worse for me.

Still easily pulled there like a moth to a flame,
I'm so angry … This is so lame.

The Anger

Anger has come to my door.
Let it in? What for?

All I see is trouble with a capital T
To allow this anger to be present in me.

Remembering the past brings hurt, I know,
And from that I have felt low.

But anger isn't something I want to meet
As I walk through a crowded street.

So when it rears its ugly head,
I want to stuff it deep inside instead.

But not letting myself have this feeling
Only postpones the much-needed healing.

So, God, I turn this over to you.
It's way bigger than anything I can do.

The Judgment

"Do you feel judged?" she asked out of the blue.
The honest reply came without much ado.

"Yes," I said, feeling some shame.
I don't really know why or from where it came.

To not understand the origin of this feeling
Continues to keep my spirit reeling.

Feeling guilty for having it is also a part
Of this lingering pain inside my heart.

"You won't understand," keeps coming to mind,
Solidifying judgment, the all-too-familiar double bind.

The Raging Tiger

It's not just anger; it's closer to rage,
Like a how a tiger feels trapped in a cage,

Nervously pacing back and forth in wait
For its keeper to open the gate.

Let me out, it cries.
I have been trapped for too long.
This exile is so very wrong.

I am tired of this captivity;
It is not a natural state for me.

I want to run free,
To be what I was meant to be.

A new freedom and a new happiness is promised for those who wait
For the master to open wide the gate.

The Misunderstanding

The conversation began with the of best intentions, or so I thought.
But when it took an ugly turn, I became distraught.

I was honest about feeling angry and let it show,
Hoping our relationship was strong enough to withstand the emotional
blow.

My chest got tight as I fought back the tears
With the intensity of feeling like I hadn't cried in years.

After an hour of talking, we finally worked it out.
Sheer exhaustion quickly followed the difficult bout.

As the day goes on, I continue to fret.
I guess I'm not up for this level of conflict yet.

The thought of drinking the pain away crosses my mind,
An ever-present reminder that I am still so inclined.

The Dear Friend

Your absence was a revelation in July.
Was I too much? Is that why?

I expected my dear friend to care,
But when I reached out, you weren't there.

Setting my own abandonment issues aside.
Like me, do you have the need to hide?

Now what to think since almost a year has passed.
Will this nagging resentment last?

The Shunning

What has changed so suddenly,
That you don't even look at me?

I used to think I knew you,
But now I don't have a clue.

Are you too busy to care how I feel?
I came to believe you were the real deal.

But unfortunately, it appears I was sadly mistaken.
Oh, how I hate feeling lost and forsaken!

The insidious refrain rings out: "I must have done something wrong."
Whisperings deep within me echo back, "See? you don't really belong."

The Confusion

I had a conversation with confusion today,
Reluctantly listened to what it had to say.

Together we developed a course of action,
Which gave me some hope and a bit of satisfaction.

It involves honesty, openness, and willingness on my part.
Still feeling a bit scared to bear my heart,

But not so much as I was before.
Very thankful the intense fear exists no more.

How things will ultimately turn out is still murky and unclear.
Praying for the ability to keep God near.

The Distraction

Where have you been these last few years,
That you have not seen my silent tears?

Do you not care what happens to me?
Are you that blind that you cannot see?

Or have you been driven to distraction,
Which will eventually cause a chain reaction,

The perfect storm demolishing everything in its wake?
This fear is way more than I can take.

The Secret

I will not cover up what's going on;
It absolutely won't help anyone.

We need each other to figure it out;
It's not only yours to talk about.

So please don't hide the truth from me.
I'm young but can clearly see

That something is very wrong,
And my fears list is quite long.

Please, oh please, be direct and honest with me,
For the truth will set both of us free.

The Limit

No more loss—I can't bare it!
Done with that; I've hit my limit.

Feeling tired, irritable, discontent.
Really don't want to be this bent.

Not ready to risk another fall.
No, not ready, not at all,

To jump back into that level of trust
Just because someone else thinks I must.

Perhaps I need to go through some pain
Before I risk my heart again.

"Easy does it" comes to mind
As I work through this current bind.

I am hoping to give God control,
Praying my creator will soothe my soul.

The Fears

Lord, I am worried and ask for courage to face what is ahead of me,
Knowing what will be, will be.

I wait with anticipation to this new day,
Praying everything will be okay.

Fear is such a powerful feeling,
It keeps me in bondage with my head reeling.

Even with the wisdom of my years,
I don't know what to do with all these fears.

It feels like I'm back at age two:
Then, I really didn't know what to do.

I was way too little to understand
That you, Jesus, had my hand.

And you have never let it go!

Dealing with Emotions: Grief and Loss

Jesus wept.

—John 11:35

I've had my share of losses, starting in my early childhood. My father served in World War II and had many traumatic experiences. As a result, he began drinking excessively and developed depression. Today, he likely would have been diagnosed with PTSD. After discharge, he remained quite ill and was in and out of the VA hospital. As a child, I saw him come home for a few months, gradually destabilize, and then leave again for months at a time. My mother was my primary caregiver, and I was very close to her. My mother died of cancer when I was sixteen and she was fifty-six. I truly believe the stress of having a very sick spouse caught up with her and took her at that young age.

Loss leads to fear of loss. In my experience, the past does not stay in the past unless it is explored and processed. I've wanted to shut the door on my past and not talk about it. That strategy did not work. I was very much in denial about how much unresolved grief and loss I was carrying. Once I because aware of this, I needed to go through the difficult process of healing the wounds. Everyone has a past with which they need to reckon.

I also struggled with loss because my husband and I dealt with infertility. Infertility treatments produced no results. I experienced feelings of unfairness. Other women were able to do this, so why couldn't I? Why did we have to be different? This grief eventually turned to great blessing because we were able to adopt three beautiful children.

The Loss

Mother, father, grandparents, friends—the litany of people dear.
For all my loved ones, I still have many unshed tears.

Past loss of support from those still with me
Is a resentment I continue to carry.

Fears of forgetting things ever linger;
The reason on which I cannot put a finger.

What is left when things are going well
Is anticipation of future loss ... Only time will tell.

It's a feeling I can't seem to shake,
Not sure exactly what it will take.

The gift of birthing a child a dream lost in the wind,
Forever wondering if I somehow had sinned.

"But then," my beautiful daughter said quietly,
"If that was meant to be, you wouldn't have me."

Now, that got my attention—
The mere timing of that mention.

Like rocks tumbling with the sand,
Transforming by the river's hand,

So too perhaps my view can slowly change
To see my losses as becoming gain.

The Grieving

Ever lurking is the fear of losing what I have gained,
Residual effect of the past losses I've sustained.

It often comes up in unexpected ways,
A reminder of the past in antique displays.

A story about the transformation of a dragonfly
Told at the church service makes me cry.

A memory of my mother, as told by my brother,
Causes a twinge of sadness like no other.

I wish I could just finally release all this pain
That gets triggered deep inside my brain.

Feelings frozen from years of repressing
Likely takes just as many years of addressing.

It's been a slow, arduous journey to become whole.
I hope patience and trust in the process will continue to heal my soul.

The Memory

The memory is still so clouded and blocked;
It feels like moving a huge mountain of rock.

A Christmas decoration from my childhood home
Reveals an unexpected but familiar path to roam.

It bids me to go where I don't want to go:
A destination I fear may take me too low.

A place of feeling underneath the protection of thought.
Something tells me there is still danger, and I will get caught

In the spiderweb that will entrap
With its impending death wrap.

Anticipation of the torment that will surely come;
I just don't know when or how or where from.

The Tears

My tears are elusive little creatures with a mind of their own.
They like to hide from all the pain that has been sown.

Desperately wanting them to bring relief
As I long to be rid of this lasting grief.

But alas, I can't seem to cry
No matter how hard I try.

So frustrated that this is not within my control,
Knowing I am truly powerless to force the goal.

Jealous of those who can express themselves this way,
I can only hope this ability will be restored someday.

Just another loss of something, so healing
Further sustains the pain I'm feeling.

The Broken Heart

My heart alone could not contain
All the years of bottled-up pain.

It oozed out in subtle ways,
Insidiously covered with thick haze.

Hidden so others could not see
What was going on with me.

I thought the past should stay the past,
And the pain would forever last.

But that seemingly was not meant to be.
The rest of the story is so much bigger than me.

Now, another chapter has begun.
Hoping in this one, I'm going to have more fun.

The Steel

My heart feels like it is encased in steel
With a strong layer of protection so I don't have to feel.

Guarding against the pain of loss is its aim.
A noble purpose; thus hard to place blame.

Although the armor may seem at times very safe,
It also feels like a tomb from which there is no escape.

This shielding against possible loss and rejection
Prevents the opportunity for real connection.

The dull ache inside screams, "Let me out!"
But the unyielding steel remains, no matter how loud the shout.

LET YOUR LIGHT SHINE
lustrare to illuminate, fr. L. lustrare.]
2. Brightness; glitter. 3. Splend
of his name. 4
1. Shining; brilliant; bright. 2
illuminated, as a room. 3. Enlightened; also
easily understood; as, a luminous explanation
lu'mi·nous·ly, adv. — lu'mi·nous·ness, n.

Finding Identity

Owning our story can be hard but not nearly as difficult
as spending our lives running from it. Only when we are
brave enough to explore the darkness will we discover the
infinite power of our light.

—Brene Brown, *The Gifts of Imperfection*[3]

At first, I didn't want to look at my story. When I finally became willing, it was an extensive search to find myself. I was an expert at putting on a mask and trying to be what I thought I should be in each area of my life. I don't think I knew who I really was deep down before. And I'm not sure I liked who I was. I had a lot of shame around being an addict. I came to the realization that I used whatever I could to not feel vulnerable, including overworking, alcohol, caretaking, and overeating.

I needed a lot of support but felt too high-maintenance to reach out. I stuffed the feelings of needing help and being vulnerable deep down. This equaled needs not being met, which led to more feelings of neediness—a double bind.

I was very afraid of rejection, and this kept me from not reaching out when I needed to do so. My lament was, "Others can work a lot and drink and not have the consequences I am experiencing." I felt different, set apart. At the same time, I experienced a growing awareness that I was so much more than what I did for a living. It was liberating!

Today, I can say with 100 percent certainty that I like myself. Not for who I am supposed to be, not for who someone else thinks I should be, and not for who I think someone else wants me to be. I like myself for who God made me to be. I have come to see that there is joy in the journey of discovering who I am and what I value. After awareness comes the important, lifelong task of being true to these values in my words and actions. The lyrics from the Song "No Longer Slaves" by Bethel Music resonates deep in my soul: "I'm no longer a slave to fear, I am a Child of God[4]."

The Middle

I've always felt stuck in the middle
Ever since I was very little.

Being everywhere and nowhere best describes the feeling—
A bitter loneliness in desperate need of healing.

Is this the destiny of the lost child, of one on the fringe,
Never wanting to hurt or impinge?

Continually wanting all strife to cease,
A burning desire to connect dots and restore peace.

A diplomat from the very start.
Is this how I should share my heart?

The desire to control the outcome often gets in my way,
And the feeling of failure is the price I pay.

Forever seeing conflict as a burden, am I willing to see the blessing in disguise?
For it can be in the search for resolution that one finds the prize.

The Drive

The drive to my destination reveals much in the morning.
Wisdom from an unknown source comes without warning.

The freshness of a new day, revelation hard to explain,
Becomes the healing balm for some of my pain.

It's been going on for about a year,
This inspiration drawing near.

It's more expansive than mere thought,
More like feelings I'm being taught.

To be true to myself, you say,
Is ultimate the goal for the day.

So on God will I depend
When I'm at my journey's end.

The Gifts

The gifts of faith, hope, and love, we are told,
Are a thousand times more precious than gold.

How about awareness, gratitude, and connection?
These are great gifts of redemption.

Then like water from a fire hose
Comes this unexpected gift of prose.

That this was possible, who knew?
I for one didn't have a clue.

What a difference a year can make,
And this last one certainly took the cake!

So thankful for the many gifts I have received.
God, this is way more than I could have ever conceived!

The Fence Sitter

I often ride the fence until my bottom is sore.
I now know the underlying truth: it's not just lore.

On middle ground I do belong, and not just because I'm trying to please.
That core belief has certainly been a big tease.

Instead, the reason is because I have been gifted to look beyond
The many perceived differences and see a common bond.

If I look past them and listen to God's call,
I will have a share in humanity after all.

The Hearts

Hearts in bondage, with crushing chains of fear and doubt,
Need the keys of faith and hope to let love out.

Jesus creates hearts that are pure,
Spirits that are steadfast and true.

May we be filled to overflowing with his love,
Willing to share this precious gift from above.

The Holy Hunger

Hungry to feel your presence, glorify your name,
I lift my hands and voice without shame.

With my face down on the floor,
Worshipping you is what I was made for.

There are times you come in quiet and solitude,
A gentle, loving interlude.

This ache in my heart I cannot deny,
Knowing only the bread of life will satisfy.

Ever longing to feel my spirit soar.
Jesus, my Lord, my savior,
I want more.

Staying the Course

It is for freedom that Christ has set us free. Stand firm, then, and do not let yourselves be burdened again by a yoke of slavery.

—Galatians 5:1

I have often pondered how to stay motivated after the newness of something wears off. I tend to jump in to a new project or process with both feet and then get bored, lose momentum, and want to quit. All or nothing—this has been a pattern throughout my life. I'm a very curious person, and once my curiosity is satisfied, I want to move on to the next interesting thing. In recovery, awareness of my traits is important to make changes as needed in order to stay the course. If something isn't working anymore, especially when a slip or relapse occurs, I need a course correction to get back on track.

My experience with relapse started with an unexpected encounter with communion wine, which started the craving cycle and a brief return to drinking. The following is an excerpt from my journal before it happened.

Hi, Dragon, let's talk. I know what you are here for. I didn't want to stir you up really, but you are awake now. Forgive the disturbance. How can I help you go back to sleep? Or is it worth the effort? I like being a sober girl; it's been two plus years, and it fits well. But now there is you tempting me, trying to pull me away from the group with wondering and questions and curiosity: "What would it be like? Aren't you curious?" Seduction is a short-lived pleasure.

Fortunately, the relapse was short-lived, and I was able to quickly get back on track. I was told that I was very lucky because others who have relapsed were not so fortunate. The key was my willingness to follow the directions of my support system to find my way back to sobriety. Finding sobriety doesn't happen overnight, and staying in recovery requires patience, endurance, and perseverance.

The Goal

My medallion says, "To thine own self be true."
This is indeed what I am striving to do.

Aware, as I begin each new day,
That barriers may block my way.

The opponents will continue to dole out their toll.
Still, I must press on towards the goal.

Perseverance is the key
For what is ultimately meant to be.

The Tiredness

This tiredness is a vivid reminder of my illness not long ago,
And I am fearful that it will keep me feeling low.

Hopefully after a few days rest, I will rebound.
To take good care of myself is the only remedy I've found.

I have this habit of comparing myself to my honey,
Whose stamina is like the Energizer bunny.

Around the house, I watch him run to and fro,
Which just strengthens the profound undertow.

Fear of judgment is what I'm feeling.
Can I be willing to trust my way of healing?

The Bad Day

I will be glad when this day is done,
So tomorrow I can begin again from square one.

Nothing seems to help my mood;
All I want to do is brood.

It is so tempting to become withdrawn.
Not any one thing I can put my finger on.

Looking for the root cause feels somewhat useful,
But bottom line this analysis isn't fruitful.

So how about I end and say
It was just a really bad day?

The Trust

"I don't trust them," I exclaim.
What new torture is lurking to dole out pain?

The phrase "one step forward and two steps back"
Somehow plays into this trust I still lack.

Hope dangled out there and then quickly snatched away.
Ha ha I got you. You thought you weren't going to have to pay!

Sounds unnervingly familiar, a major tease.
I question God, "Who I am trying to appease?"

My inner voice says that deep healing has commenced—
A gift I should try to embrace and not fight against.

But this journey is so hard, I cry.
I feel so alone; sometimes I just want to die.

Sorrow unable be consoled.
Dear God, this grief feels very old.

The Sweet Spot

My pursuit continues daily for the sweet spot.
Its exact location I often know not,

For the spot continually moves and hides,
Outwardly mysterious as the oceans tides.

To find it, my creativity and intuition is the key.
But when I'm overtired, that skill eludes me.

The pain from my recent personal adventures shows the way.
Slowly coming to believe it was a small price to pay

For the deep awareness of such a simple rule:
That like a car, creativity and intuition will not work
Without proper care and the right fuel.

The Motivation

From where can motivation come when the passion isn't there?
If I'm honest, I'd admit I just really don't care.

So the day drags endlessly by,
And ugly feelings swirl and cry.

I'm lonely, I'm jealous, I'm feeling left out.
The little kid inside just wants to sit and pout.

From where can motivation come when it's no longer in your soul?
In the recent past, people pleasing was a primary goal.

That kept me engaged in the work I did.
Now, without it I feel like a little kid.

Not able to stay focused on a necessary chore,
Thinking it is a major bore.

From where can motivation come when desire to succeed wears thin?
Presuming there are no more ladders to climb in.

Feeling ignored and shelved without relief,
I can't seem to shake this painful belief.

This motivation I seek must come from a higher source,
Because I haven't been able to access it on my current course.

The Tree

Sometimes I feel like a withering tree
With thick vines that threaten to smother me.

Once strong and sturdy with branches reaching to the sky,
Today I feel small and weak and long to cry.

But crying seems to be out of my reach;
The dense briars cling to my emotions like a leech.

They cut me off from the nourishment of the sun and rain,
Leaving me with just this soul numbing pain.

Wearily I search for answers I can never seem to find
As the spreading vines continue to torment my mind.

The Shame

My heart weeps and breaks over the little one's pain;
Beautiful joy turns quickly into shame.

How can this happen so fast?
I so want the feeling to last.

There is really nothing anyone can do.
The feelings must be allowed to pass through

For this heart to fully mend.
Then the pattern of shame may eventually end.

The Blame Game

God, I don't want to be in this pain again.
Think it should be over and well on the mend.

But here it is, just the same,
As I look for something or someone to blame.

The question "Why?" is back in my mind—
And other disturbing thoughts much more unkind.

This is hurting me way more than it's hurting them,
And right now, I feel the anger will never end.

Dear Lord, please create in me a heart that's pure
And a spirit that is steadfast and sure,

So I can sincerely say, "Live and let live,"
And know that I still have much to give.

The Pieces

My spirit feels broken and tattered,
But not completely shattered.

This time I have all the pieces in plain view
And, thankfully with God's grace, know what to do.

When stress takes its toll,
I have learned to rest and nurture my soul.

I hear the confirming whisper in the quiet of the morn
That something else is waiting to be born.

In the meantime, I believe that with time the pieces will mend,
Trusting I soon will be whole again.

The Fault

It is not your fault, little one,
Another of life's lessons has begun.

Confusion and blame the insidious pair,
Reminders that life can be unfair.

When the student is ready, the teacher appears,
And there are powerful tools to calm your fears.

Use the tools of honesty, openness, and willingness,
And don't forget courage to say yes!

What's past will occasionally show up from the past.
Remember that these feelings do not last.

There will always be more to be revealed.
Believe that eventually your heart will be healed.

The Lightness

There is a noticeable lightness, an opening of my spirit.
Still, old voices in my head tell me to fear it,

Thinking it's a precursor to some catastrophe.
What does that really say about me?

Thankfully, I've increased my ability to let those thoughts pass by
Without clinging on to them or asking why.

This is the fruit of prayer and meditation,
An incredible restoration

Of a spirit broken from life's storms,
Grateful for healing that transforms.

I hear the message: "Bloom where you're planted, and let your lightness show,
As it takes rain as well as light to make flowers grow."

Connection and Belonging

Stir in me a love that's deep, a love that's wide, a love that's sweet and help me, Lord to never keep it to myself.

—Steffany Gretzinger, from the song "No Fear in Love"[5]

A cornerstone of my recovery has been connection with others who can relate and understand what I am going through. When I started my recovery journey, I had deep feelings of loneliness and disconnection from others. I would feel lonely when I was alone and when I was with other people around me. I learned through the healing process that in order to feel better, I needed to allow others into my life who could help. I had to take a hard look at my current relationships and let go of some of them that weren't healthy. That was very difficult, given my struggles with loss. I also needed to learn how to effectively deal with conflict.

As with anything new, it takes practice and effort. To get to a place where I felt connected to others required getting out of my comfort zone, reaching out, and asking for help. It required taking the risk of vulnerability. I could not have done it without the people in my life. This connection with people initially took the form of group therapy, individual therapy, and self-help groups. Once I found people whom I felt a connection with, I was able to build my support network. I can't stress enough how important this was and continues to be. When we share ourselves with others, they are more likely to share with us. It is very healing to sit with others who can relate to my story. This is beneficial for the person who needs help, as well as the person who is available to help. It is amazing to have the desire to pay it forward and be there for others as others were there for me.

The Rooms

I feel much stronger than I did a year ago.
In these rooms, receiving what I need to heal and grow.

Connection with my fellows traveling along the same road
Has lightened the heavy burdensome load

That I've been carrying most of my life,
A source of much pain, turmoil, and strife.

Sharing our stories inspire who we are meant to be
As we continue together on our journey of recovery.

The Sponsor

I was so scared to ask someone to sponsor me.
Didn't think anyone would take the job, you see.

Or if they did, it wouldn't work out.
So why put myself through all that doubt?

Best I don't ask at all,
So I don't risk taking a fall.

But then I heard "Courage in the face of fear"
Whispered in my other ear.

"Be willing to let go and fly.
You'll never know until you try."

It all came together one morning.
I asked for the support without warning.

She said yes without delay
And really made my day!

The Coffee

Drinking coffee has become a way of connecting,
A simple catalyst for reflecting

On life's challenges and opportunities
With myself, friends, and family.

The pondering and intimate conversations that ensue
Are platforms for my tattered spirit to renew.

That first smell of coffee as I arise
Gives an instant burst of energy with no surprise.

Walking into a familiar coffee shop during the day
Can recolor my mood out of gray.

Thank you, coffee, for all that you do.
You are indeed a pleasurable brew.

The Present

Learning to live in the present is elusive.
This insight remains quite conclusive.

To project into the future or dwell in the past
Will keep us stuck, feeling downcast.

Change is unavoidable,
And what will come, only time will tell.

In the meantime, I am choosing to embrace what is,
Because in the now is where joy lives.

So when you change the subject, fidget, or look away,
You subtly keep this connection at bay.

I will try to be present for you when need be.
Can you be here right now for me?

The Best Friend

I am so grateful for my best friend.
With you, I don't have to pretend.
Who I am and who I'm not.
That means quite a lot

To a person who all her life has been hiding behind a wall,
So afraid of the tremendous fall.

Old fears of abandonment and rejection
Are replaced by feelings of support and protection.

Thank you, my friend, for being there.
I can tell you really do care!

The Homecoming

Yes, I am glad to be home.
No more do I have to roam.

As I look around the table in St. Croix,
I embrace my friends with great joy.

Belonging—the feeling is like no other,
For these are true sisters and brothers.

This is one of the most amazing miracles I have ever known,
For God is doing for me what I could not do alone.

He has granted me my deepest longing,
This incredible gift of belonging.

Not the way I ever dreamed,
For surprises have been his theme.

Yes, I am truly home.
No more do I have to roam.

The Angel

When I needed her, she was there.
For this I offer up a heartfelt prayer.

All I had to do was ask.
Asking sure can be a difficult task!

For I've had many doubts and fears
That have haunted me across the years.

Disappointment, abandonment, rejection, loss, and shame—
That's been the name of the game.

Yet here was God's representative from heaven above.
So very grateful to feel her love.

Yet another of many signs showing that I have nothing to fear.
Thank you, God, for this angel dear.

The Flowers

Thank you, God, for all the amazing women in my life.
Beautiful flowers in a stunning bouquet,
Each one special and unique,
Filling my soul,
Satisfying my hunger,
Meeting my need
For acceptance,
For belonging,
For connection.

The Cheeseburger

When I share something personal,
Your attempt to be funny doesn't sit well.

Is it because I also try to laugh it off?
A half-hearted way to express myself.

And then you don't know what to do,
So you join in the joking too?

There is a fine line between lightening the mood
And biting sarcasm that reveals an attitude.

This realization came this morning,
Clarity that may be transforming.

If I don't laugh, I may just cry,
And then I'll need to explain why.

My goal is to share real feelings
So we can continue healing.

But it's so hard to take off this mask;
Likely going to be a lifelong task.

So how do I tell you this
Without putting you or me in a shame abyss?

Maybe some evening as I'm with you, dear,
I can share this without fear.

The Weeding

Our current conflicts feel like weeds in an untended garden
As lingering resentments cause our hearts to harden.

Fortunately, like weeding, after all the initial cleanup work is done,
It will take far less struggle and concentrated time in the long run.

We've been down this path a ways before,
Only to come back to the beginning once more.

A maintenance strategy is what we need,
A simple plan to help us succeed.

Commitment to daily connection on things of import
Will be our key catalyst for relationship support.

grace in every moment

I AM in the PRESENCE of the LORD!

Trusting God

I will trust, here in the mystery.

—Amanda Cook, "Heroes"[6]

I am learning to trust God more every day. It has and continues to be a journey, not a destination. I've struggled with trust issues throughout my life, especially with trusting authority figures. This fear can get in the way of trusting the ultimate authority of the universe.

In the past, I've been so mad at God that I denied his existence. My justification was, "This bad thing happened, and so therefore God doesn't exist." I still have residual feelings of anger that crops up from time to time. Now I can recognize it as anger and address it with him in a constructive manner.

Increasing my trust in God has been and continues to be a process of surrender. When a logical answer is not available, I tend to spin it around in my head, trying to figure it out. I struggle most when I'm waiting for something important to me. I have a strong desire to know the outcome or the destination. "I am responsible for the effort and not the outcome" is a helpful slogan that I heard from others in recovery. I am asked to do my part, wait on the Lord, and trust that he is faithful and will give me what I need.

By the grace of God, I am learning to say, "I don't know why this is happening, and I may never know." I then pray for knowledge of God's will for me and for the power to carry that out.

The Waiting

Lately it has been so hard to wait, like patience has ceased to exist,
Replaced by a desire for instant gratification that continues to persist.

Where is she? It needs to happen now. I can't wait. Why is it taking so long?
These are the familiar stanzas of an addict's song.

To be at peace with this state is not an easy goal,
One that requires me to rigorously search my soul

For the fragile trust hiding under fear and doubt,
Masked by the facade of believing I have the timing all figured out.

Waiting convinces me that my prayers aren't heard, that's true.
So, God, I'm willing to be willing to turn over the timetable to you.

The Promises

In the past, I read the promises, thinking "Could they really apply to me?"
"Oh, God, help me to trust you," was my desperate plea.

Astonished as I read the promises now:
Many of them are being fulfilled somehow.

Complete trust in God still feels like an impossible goal,
Something that might just fill the insatiable hole.

Until that happens, I am willing to do my part and stay the course,
With the knowledge that of this transformation, I am not the ultimate
source.

I cannot deny that the promises are slowly coming true—
Further evidence that maybe, God, I can trust you!

The Slipping

I've slowly slipped off the edge
And now find myself dangling from a high ledge.

My body feels like it weighs a ton.
Praying for help before my fingers release one by one.

I strain to hear an encouraging call.
I am so afraid of the fall.

As I listen to the voices,
There are only two choices.

Hang on. Let go.
But what lies below?

Fear has me mesmerized.
I just may be surprised.

Is it possible that I won't fall but fly?
What would happen if I let go and try?

But knowledge tells me I am not a bird.
To assume I've somehow grown wings is absurd.

The only option is to hold on tight
And hope God will make it all right.

The Willingness

Dear Lord, I do want to believe
That you will give me a reprieve.

From this insanity that has returned my way,
What price now do I have to pay?

I can't do this anymore;
It feels like a big festering sore.

Something has got to give
To allow me to truly live.

And yet this night, I suffer alone.
It's really no fault of my own.

As waves of nausea wash over me, I get miffed.
I refuse to be a victim to this!

Then suddenly I realize I am on my knees.
Humility paired with willingness are the keys.

Do with me as you can.
I am ready to surrender to your plan.

The Ultimate Sponsor

I'm still so very shaken and sad,
And feeling a bit mad.

Perhaps I can find another one
When this grieving at last is done.

In the meantime, I asked God to sponsor me.
He said, "Yes, of course," with glee.

And then a thought followed suddenly.
My dear, what a beautiful step three!

Can I view this as a time to grow?
Strengthening my ability to go

To this place of uncertainty and fear
And truly know that God is near?

The Flight

Before I go down a certain runway,
I usually want to know the flight path today.

That's not how it works, my child.
At times this trip will be kind of wild.

I promise to keep you in my care,
Safe and sound without too many a scare.

Just stay open and follow the signs along the way.
I will give you all you need each day.

The choices will become clear;
Try not to travel with fear.

There is no need for a huge revelation
To arrive safely at your destination.

The Challenge

Let God use me without consulting me.
May I be open to this challenging opportunity.

An adventure suited for both the courageous and the meek,
Perhaps a path to the joy we all seek.

My desire to know what's at the end of the road
Can become a very heavy load.

Fear can also keep me stuck
Unable to move through the muck.

And yet a gentle voice whispers, "One step at a time, my dear.
Be willing to keep moving despite the fear.

For my yoke is easy and my burden light.
In time, you will know what path is right."

The Sadness

Something I really wanted has slipped away.
Being rigorously honest has a price to pay.

My heart said it was the right thing to do,
Even though my head could justify not doing it too.

I carry on with feelings
Of disappointment and loss tinged with a bit of shame,
Aware that personal integrity is the name of the game.

Knowing that time will heal the lingering pain,
Hoping the opportunity will come again.

Waiting for my creator to give the nod,
I turn the timetable over to God.

The Guardian

May she be there to protect and guide you
When you don't know what to do.

May she be a beacon of hope and light
When you are lost in the dark of night.

May she give you strength when you feel weak,
For God blesses the humble and the meek.

May she give you peace when you are mad.
May she shower you with joy when you are sad.

May she give you shelter from the storm
When chaos feels like the norm.

May she give you courage in the face of fear
To take right action despite the jeer.

May God's grace that comes from above
Shine through her with faith and love.

May you always feel her near,
This precious guardian dear.

The Words

"Behold, I make all things new.
Write these words down for they are trustworthy and true."

With intense anticipation, I write them down
As my mouth curls into a frown.

This familiar pain I know all too well:
Trying to force the answer when only time will tell.

Why, Lord, do I struggle so hard to just trust and believe?
Is there any way I can get a reprieve?

"Patience, my dear," is the whisper I hear.
"Continue your willingness to serve despite the fear.

In this moment your struggle has a purpose of its own.
At the right time, this too will be known."

The Rock

With a weary heart, I peer into the pond
As I request help from the great beyond.

I want to let it go, but fear keeps the heavy rock in my hand.
When will I trust you, God, and surrender totally to your plan?

Why am I holding on still?
How do I let go of my will?

"Please, Lord, replace this fear with courage," I pray.
A gentle whisper comes without delay.

"Just trust and jump in, rock and all.
Believe into my loving arms you will fall."

With increased faith, I decide to take the leap
And with a big splash plunge into the deep.

The Vows

Based on Psalm 37:5–7

Prophets foretold of his birth.
"Come now, long-expected Jesus," was their cry on earth.

And he promised he would come again.
These are my vows until then.

I will commit my ways to you,
Trust that your word is true.

Let integrity be my guide,
And fairness shine like the sun at noontide.

Be still before your throne,
Act when your will is known.

SHE KNOWS WHERE THE LIGHT IS

Gratitude and Courage

Courage doesn't always roar. Sometimes courage is the quiet
voice at the end of the day saying, "I will try again tomorrow."

—Mary Anne Radmacher[7]

I am so grateful for the transformation that has happened in my life. I wasn't grateful at the start of my recovery, and this feeling of gratitude didn't happen overnight. It takes time and practice to cultivate an attitude of gratitude. When I'm having a bad day, I try to focus my thoughts on the positives in my life. Early in my recovery, it was suggested that I write a gratitude list to help me remember what I have.

It takes courage to change, and courage to show up and do the work. I was told when I stepped into recovery that there would be so many wonderful changes I would experience.

Initially I did not believe change was possible for me; it felt too out of reach. I am grateful and amazed that I can claim every one of the promised changes today. I feel a new freedom and happiness, an authenticity. I feel I have something to contribute. I feel I have a place and a role in the world. I feel God has a plan for me. My poem "The Abundance" reflects this change of attitude and desire of wanting to share this gift with others. My constant prayer is for the Lord to show me how to love. I ask for courage to respond out of love and to not stay silent if my words or actions will help another. It takes courage to step out in faith and trust that God has the best plan for our lives.

The Change

Mother's Day again, and what a change.
Not long ago, I was in a place very strange.

A realization I needed help, but didn't have a clue
What I was going to do.

I hit a bottom, reached out, and bared my heart.
As hard as that was, it gave me a start.

Beginning a journey to the solution,
I took a shaky step toward resolution.

What a challenging year it has been,
So incredibly far beyond my ken.

Fast forward to this day.
It really was a small price to pay.

Grateful for the many gifts I've received,
And for healing not yet perceived.

It is often said that growth comes from pain.
I'm glad to witness there has been tremendous gain.

Because the amazing place I'm in today
Is the place I want to stay!

The Helper

A year ago today,
A fellow traveler helped me along the way.

As I sit here gazing at the place
Where my healing began,
I am reminded just how lucky I am

To be a part of this journey of recovery,
Each new day an adventure of discovery.

I am so grateful to the helper
Who took time to grant me shelter

From the storm of life that was blowing.
Who knew where it was all going?

I hope someday I can return the good deed
For another fellow traveler in need.

The Gratitude

Waves of gratitude flood over me.
So thankful for a new sense of who I'm meant to be.

Amazed by all the people that have come into my life
To support my journey out of pain and strife.

Random calls from friends out of the blue
Brings a joy I never knew.

A curious skill of knowing when to go with the flow
And not fight with the strong undertow.

The ability to believe my inner voice
Gives me reason to rejoice.

The newfound gift of creativity
Pairs with the desire for spontaneity,

The confidence to speak my heart's song
With the emerging belief that I belong.

Grateful for the courage to approach life one day at a time.
Who knew this journey could be so sublime?

The Six Aspirations

May I continue to believe that I am not alone,
Grateful that the gift of belonging is now being known.

May I be patient amid life's difficulties,
Confident of the return of calmer seas.

May I look fear in the face,
Putting courage in first place.

May I live with ease,
Only the present moment to appease.

May I trust that my Lord has my back,
Taking care of the things I lack.

May I embrace what I've been gifted to do.
Oh, world, help me to be of service to you!

The Strawberry

To embrace what is and not worry about what is to be—
What an amazing gift of freedom this is for me.

A wondrous place that feels very much like home.
No longer do I have the need to roam.

The tigers will always be there,
And the strawberries are usually rare.

When the opportunity to taste one appears,
I now have the wisdom of my years

To take what has been placed in my path
With sincere gratitude instead of wrath.

I vow to continue giving life the best I can
And trust that God has the best plan.

The Abundance

My heart overflows with love.
This precious gift can only come from above.

For a long time, I've been in a place of scarcity,
A feeling all too familiar to me.

Now, I find myself in a place of abundance and generosity
And want to give what I have to people I see.

This abundance is not financial gain
But a much bigger gift to obtain

A wondrous change of mind and heart,
An increasing desire to do my part

So that others can truly live.
Grateful to believe I have much to give.

The Armor

Based on Ephesians 6:13–17

There are so many needs, is my lament.
How can I possibly care for those to whom I am sent?

It takes willingness to help just one today, came the reply.
And some practice in letting go of the overwhelming question of why.

Truth, faith, prayer, perseverance, are elements in the armor of protection
To fight the huge waves of fear, doubt, and indecision.

Believe that confusion fear and doubt cannot abide
With courage, prayer, fellowship, and grit on your side.

Put on the armor of God; that is the first thing to do.
And then rest assured the power will be given to you.

The Shattering

Based on 2 Timothy 1:7

Fear shattered this heart, making it cower.
Now God holds the pieces together with love and power.

Grateful the Lord is ever near.
My heart is no longer a slave to fear.

The Season

Waiting impatiently for the reason,
Remembering for everything there is a season.

Struggling with the desire to put God to the test,
Longing for clear proof this vision is not in jest,
Praying for peace and clarity on this quest.

Becoming willing to expose my soul,
Risking disappointment and rejection to pursue the goal.

Thanking God for the gift of time
To create inspiring prose and rhyme.

Choosing to believe this blessing is the real deal,
Joining together to help others heal.

Notes

1   Bryan E. Robinson, *Work Addiction: Hidden Legacies of Adult Children* (Deerfield Beach: Health Communications, Inc., 1989).

2   Karen Casey, *Each Day a New Beginning: Daily Meditations for Women* (Center City: Hazelden, 1991).

3   Brene C. Brown, *The Gifts of Imperfection* (Center City: Hazelden, 2010).

4   J. Helser, Joel Case, and Brian Johnson, "No Longer Slaves," *We Will Not Be Shaken* (Bethel Music Publishing, 2014).

5   S. Gretzinger and Nate Ward, "No Fear in Love," *The Undoing* (Bethel Music Publishing, 2014).

6   A. Cook, Jason Ingram, and Paul Mabury, "Heroes," *Brave New World,* (Bethel Music Publishing, 2015).

7   Mary Anne Radmacher, *Courage Doesn't Always Roar* (San Francisco: Conari Press, 2009).

Printed and bound by PG in the USA

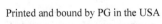